Crip Lyrics
The Unapologetic Poetry of Disability

Val Vera

POOR Press

Crip Lyrics: The Unapologetic Poetry of Disability is a collection of poems framing the many facets of Disability Culture. Written by disabled activist, speaker, organizer, and writer Val Vera, ***Crip Lyrics*** unveils the author's lived experiences and visceral connection with his identity as a "Crip" - a controversial yet widely used term adopted by the unapologetic voices within the Disability Community. Masterfully illustrated by disabled artist Melissa Marie Eckardt, ***Crip Lyrics*** boldly displays the art of Disability.

About the Author

Val Vera is a Disability Justice activist, speaker, organizer and writer. Originally from Chicago, Val began his Disability Justice career in San Diego and has served on several boards focused on disability culture and equity. His intersectional experience as a Disabled Latinx, coupled with his Disability Justice work, is revealed by the imagery and passion in his writing.

Val currently lives in Denton, TX where he organizes, educates and serves with the local Disability Community. He is an avid moviegoer, music lover and sports aficionado. Above all, Val enjoys laughing and spending unscripted time with his favorite person Michelle.

ISBN 978-1-956534-01-6

Thank you to POOR Press team for design and copy-editing.

A POOR Press Publication © 2021. All Rights Reserved.

POOR Press is a poor and indigenous people-led press dedicated to publishing the books and scholarship of youth, adults, and elders in poverty locally and globally.

www.poormagazine.org
www.poorpress.net

Contents

Part One: *Pride, Identity, and the Taboo Subject Thing*

    Chair Thing   7

    Skin   9

    Entirety   11

    My Cripple   13

    Wretched Pain   15

    Voids   17

    Let 'em Know   19

    Lascivious Grin   21

    This Body   23

Part Two: *Crip Justice and the Oil-bathed Hands*

    Worthy   27

    Not Your Granddaddy's Crip   29

    Kneel   31

    Crip Appropriation … *or* Crip Uprising … *or* Abled Karens at it Again   33

    Creation   35

    Healed   37

    Dark Side   39

Part Three: *Dreams, Death, and Visceral Verses*

    Crip Paradise   43

    Walls   45

    You, not me   47

    Dear Young Me   49

    Last Breath   53

    Unburied   55

Part One

Pride, Identity, and the Taboo Subject Thing

Chair Thing

So, this chair thing
This, you're kind of scared thing
This eye-catching, make you stare thing
The thought-prompting, curiosity-leading,
Cause you to wonder thing
Let me answer your everything

Your,
I never knew thing …
I kind of figured thing…
I had no idea thing…
I have a… fascination thing
The, does it hurt thing
How do you put your shirt thing?
Do you flirt thing?
What about the sex thing?
The, does it get erect thing?
The taboo subject thing
The simple and complex thing
The "you wanna race?" thing
The how fast can you go? thing
The embarrassed face thing
The "how do you go?" thing

Wouldn't it be comforting
getting rid of the ignorance… thing?
The wall that blocks the knowledge thing
The key to the enlightening
So, this chair thing
The, are you ready to be aware thing
The let's stop the stare thing
The get over your scared thing

Skin

The skin I'm in.
This brown & disabled skin I'm in.

The skin you say is derived from sin.
The skin that exclaims I don't fit in!

This skin I'm in won't let me in
your abled world,
ivory within.

This skin that's rejected again and again.
"Hey, you Rican!"
"That chair can't get in!"

This skin I'm in,
a gift from Him?

My cross to bear,
my sink or swim?

This skin that fits my soulful whim.
Embraces me 'til I give in.

This skin I'm in, I love this skin.
This brown & disabled skin I'm in.

Entirety

Look at me!
No, stop and look at me!
Don't glance or peek discreetly.
Fix your eyes on what you see.

From head to toe,
my entirety.
Beyond the obvious, look deeply.
Kick down the doors of superficiality.

Now do you see, my humanity?
Clothed in my disability?

My mind that wanders occasionally.
My heart that adores so painfully.
My soul that clings to eternity.
My desires of lust and sexuality.
My cravings for fame and anonymity.
My being of simple complexity.

Now do you see?
Can you see?
Are you blinded by society?
Their views of who I'm supposed to be?
A useless image of malformity?

Perhaps it's my transparency
that makes you feel uncomfortably?
The thought of similarity?
The imperfect image of you in me?

Look at me, a really good look at me.
Do you now see the whole of me?
The fractured art made beautifully.

Now is the time to look at me.

My Cripple

My Cripple. It is me, mine, the whole of who you see.
My aura, my being, my full identity.

My Cripple is more than rubber tires, this chariot bathed in black.
Rolling on the spineless skin of ableism's back.

My Cripple is who you see when our eyes meet. Who you hear, a voice not so meek.
That awkward moment to shake its hand. My Cripple is there, disguised as man.

My Cripple feels and embraces life. Moments and memories of beauty and strife.

The sun wraps my Cripple in a soothing warm embrace.
The gentle breeze kisses my Cripple on its brown and bearded face.
The night beckons my Cripple to prowl and roam about.
The quiet reminds my Cripple of the life it lives without.

My Cripple craves.
Relationship.
Friendship.
Kinship.
It survives on spoonfuls of hardship.

Battleship.
My Cripple is armed with knowledge and skills.
Words that dissect.
Sarcasm that kills.

An appetite for lust.
Erotic.
Exotic.
Skin on skin.
My Cripple is boundless in satisfaction's sin.

My Cripple. It is me, mine, the whole of who you see.
Uniquely undefined.
Profound imagery.

Wretched Pain

Wretched pain!
The angst, the throb
This fucking throb!
Each blink,
each breath,
sinking closer to death
Death to me or death to this pain?
Are we not one and the same?
Could one leave and the other remain?

I give you shelter
I give you purpose
I give you…
Oh, these aches!
These fucking aches!
Every shift
of this frail brown body
ends in a melody of
winces and pinches
Orchestrating melancholy verses
    throughout these crippled inches

Inches that curse you
Inches that loathe you
Inches that nurse and stylishly clothe you
Inches that keep you from public's eye
Unworthy to be displayed
Unknown to those who call my name
Unheard through the sounds of life's
    mundane

Oh, but I know you!
I hear your vile voice!
I feel your jagged touch!
The throb...
This fucking throb!
These fucking aches!
Screaming through my spirit like a siren
    that wakes!
Wakes the mind to high alert
Wakes the body to experience the hurt
Wakes the soul
my Crip and Latin soul
each time it longs to touch dirt.

Stab at me endlessly
Scratch at me ritually
Pound through me relentlessly
For you
wretched pain
are my affirmation
My validation of being
My exclamation of existence
My proclamation of resistance
My dedication to persistence

Your insistence feeds my crave to survive
Wretched pain
my reminder that I am alive

Voids

I touch you with terms of endearment, affection,
a caress of attention.
A connection to your spirit, your soul.

That beautiful soul.

The way your mind tugs
on my intellect's thirst.
The rhythm of your words soothes with each verse.
Your image,
imperfectly perfect,
is what engulfs me first.

What does it feel like to be bathed in adoration's seas?
The currents of attraction pulling you deeper to me.
Your lack of resistance prompts my insistence
to shower you in lover's soliloquy.

Show me the feeling of being pursued.
Reflect the rays of adoration that shine brilliantly on you.
Fill the depths of my voids with all of you.

Every ounce of you.

I crave your interest in who I am,
what I do,
how I feel.
Ask me questions filled
with intimate intentions. Dive into my Crip wounds with a passionate heal.
Dive into my voids,
our voids,
allow them to reveal.

Voids that call for you.
Voids that call for me.
Voids that call longingly.

Let 'em Know

The attention you crave
is at your disposal.
Flowing from the fountain within my soul.
It fuels your passion,
not to be boastful.
It satisfies your whims,
unlike your past hopefuls.
Dousing your dark desires,
leaving you refreshed and vocal.
Yodel,
sing to the world!
Let 'em Know how this Crip quakes your world.
Let 'em Know that this Crip makes you twirl.
Let 'em Know I'm the Crip that owns the pearls.

I know the others don't see.
I know the others don't believe,
that a human like me brings you to your knees.
Flowing from my soul, my Crip identity,
pours the elixir that feeds your ravenous needs.
Filling your empty from those before me.

Soothing your yearning left by those before me.
Dousing your thirsty caused by those withered
    abled bodies.
Let 'em Know how this Crip does the deeds.
Let 'em Know that this Crip exceeds.
Let 'em Know I'm the Crip that supersedes.

The affection you crave is fed on the ready.
Flowing from my soul,
slow and steady.
I fuel your passion,
my confidence is heavy.
I satisfy your whims,
your past feeling envy.
I darken your desires,
heart-pounding sweaty.
Scream,
shout to the many!
Let 'em Know how this Crip hits the medley.
Let 'em Know that this Crip is dark and edgy.
Let 'em Know I'm the Crip who fills on the ready.

Lascivious Grin

Intertwined,
skin on skin.
Lost in your lips,
euphoria sets in.
Where do I end?
Where do you begin?
The art of imperfect.
Crip's perfection.
The scent of our lust.
The hymn of our sin.
The chemistry of us.
The thunder of our vim.
Passion unleashed,
a lascivious grin.
Intertwined in a pool
of intoxicating whim.

This Body

Make love to this body
Its curves and turns
the way it yearns
to be loved by somebody

Seduce this body
With eyes that look beyond imperfection
With hands and lips of resurrection
Let your tongue erase fears of rejection

Desire this body
obscured by a chair
Mouth on mine
skin on skin
Lust sublime
an escapade of sin

Fantasize of this body
embrace the rise of me
Open your mind and see
the passion explode from this body

Make love to this body
Its curves and turns
the way it yearns
to be seduced by somebody

Part Two

Crip Justice and the Oil-bathed Hands

Worthy

Worthy, we are.
Our bodies,
though different than theirs,
breathe,
move.
Yet, they disapprove.
Rejection of our existence.
Objection to our resistance.
Ableist spirits keep us at a distance.

Worthy, we are.
Yet, segregated,
isolated
from society's circles.
Their words,
actions.
Silence smothers the scarred hurtful.

Worthy, we are.
Our bodies,
though different than yours,
rise,
resist!
We will insist!
Rejection of your abled privilege.
Objection to your rabid pillage.
Crip chants loudly surround the village!

Worthy, we are.
Yes,
agitated,
aggravated
by society's circles.
Your words,
actions.
Defiance utters from the scarred worthful.
Worthy, we are!

Not Your Granddaddy's Crip

I know what you're thinking:

"You've not inspirational.
Motivational.
Warm and fuzzy sensational."

Confrontational!

That's who I am.
Fighting against oppression with these crippled hands.

Calling out privilege of the ableist man.
Posting these lyrics like Will.I.Am.

Excuse me ma'am?!

Do my words offend?
Ruining your image of a 'handicapped' friend?
Tarnishing your charity and latest trend?

I will not blend!

I do not pander.
My words are precise,
Surgical candor.

Commander!

My course is set.
Decades of injustice have now become debt.
Owed to my siblings who will not forget.
Pay it in full with fucking respect!

It's time to collect.

From institutions that segregate.
Media that manipulate.
Police who violate
With force and guns.
Creating programs so we don't run.

I'm done!

Dealing with your tricks and mixin'.
Take Me Home is your idea of fixin'.
Scheming low key like a dick named Nixon.
Wearing blood on your hands, officer Dickson?

I get my licks in!

Don't slide or slip.
Inspiration porn
will fatten your lip.
Motivation's scorn
is a tight Latin grip.
By now you should know
I'm not your grandaddy's Crip.

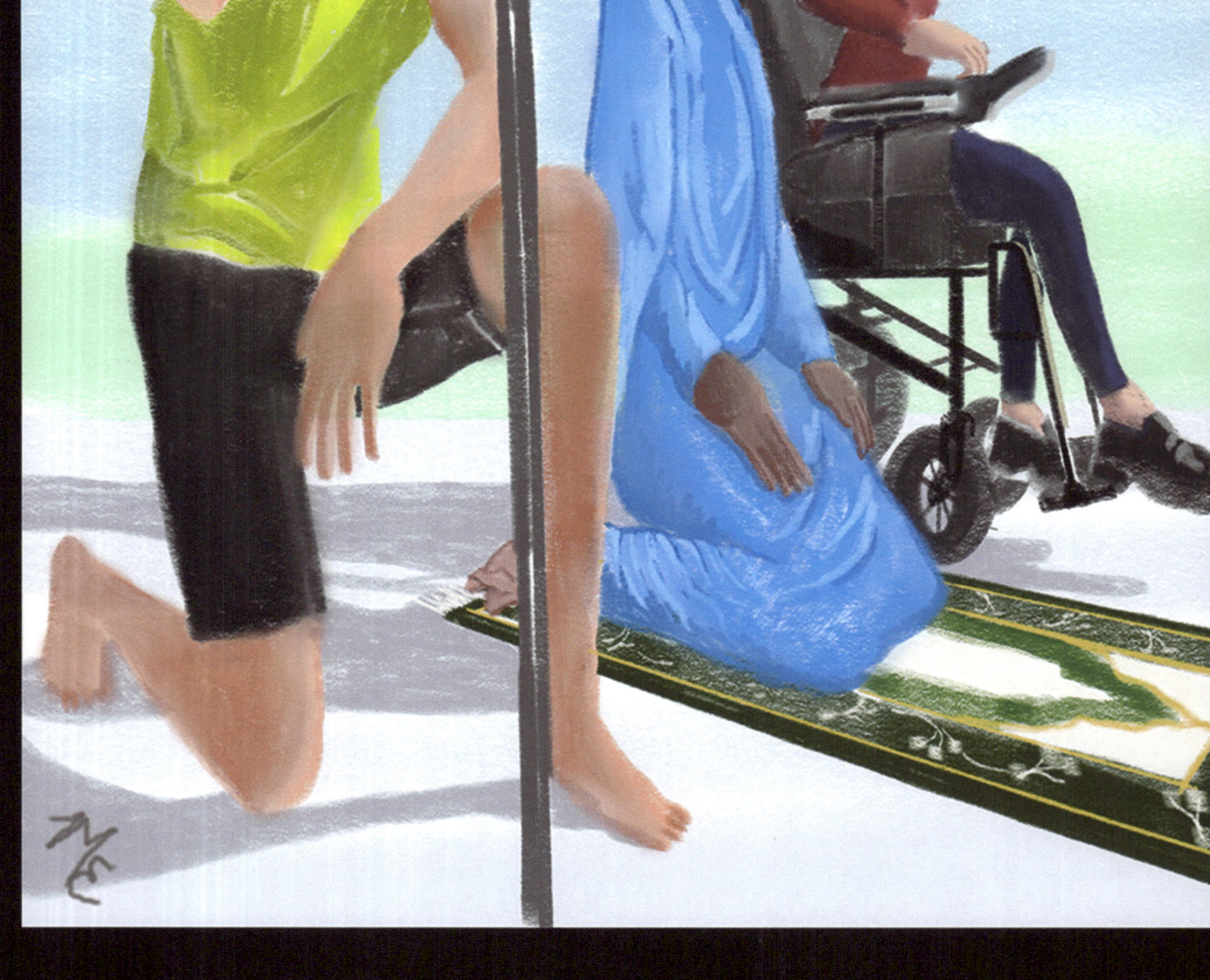

Kneel

If I could walk, I would kneel
Against atrocities, oppression, a flag of false impression

Land of the free?
If you don't look like me
Abled caucasity
The code to liberty

If I could walk, I would kneel
On the neck of isms and systems that capitalize on prisons

Cages only enrage us!
Your privilege is outrageous!
Determined to engage us through historical pages
of
Hatred.
Violence.
Voices no longer silent!

If I could walk, I would kneel
Armed for battle
Justice of steel

White Supremacy
White House Supremacist

Targets are set!
Bullets of Black fists,
Brown fists,
Native fists,
Cripple fists!
Enough of this!
Righteous anger responds like this!

Like Jesus at the temple
Turning tables
It's time to turn the tables of our temple!

Crip Appropriation
... *or*
Crip Uprising
... *or*
Abled Karens at it Again

Check them out!
The ableds are styling…
I mean stealing!
Decked out in the hottest gear.
Curated for a pandemic year.
Open your eyes and let everyone hear.

Haven't you heard?
Crip Crip Crip,
Crip is the Word!

Like orange is the new black.
Crip is the new cool.
That "too cool for school" cool.
That "new silk shirt on the abled body" cool.

Draped in Crip like a fur coat.
Checking off boxes in order to vote.
They're not trying to catch a virus.
Putting on disguises.
Pretending to be us!
Perpetrating.
Masquerading.
Crip parading!

Quit parading that handi-veil!
Claiming Crip to vote by mail!

Warm and cozy in their new Crip jammies.
Tele-working.
Tele-healthing.
Tele-living for a living.
Crips were begging for that tele life,
that curbside life,
that get-whatever-you-want-to-the-front-door life.

"Get a life" is what they said.
"If you can't get to work… get your food… get to a doc…"
"You're better off dead."
Hmmm, I wonder...
Who's living 6 feet under?
Layered in Crip clothes.
Hiding from pandemic's thunder.

Behind a mask they refuse to wear.
Strapping on the Crip Cape like Gucci underwear.
"I'm exempt!" is their battle cry.
"If I wear this mask, I'll surely die"
…"I've got handicaps I don't need to explain."
…"Underlying conditions with underlying names."

Bullshit Karen!
You've got no shame!
Getting your hair done is your aim!
Getting your nails done is your game!
Getting your abled privilege pampered is your fame!

Stealing Crip Culture
like a cowardly vulture?
It's time for OUR uprising!
Taking down abled sculptures!

I'm taking back mine!
My Crip skin that was gifted to me!
My Crip clothes that fit to a T!
My Cripness!
My Cripdom!
My Crip identity!

Creation

Look what you've done,
what you've created
Quiet poster child turned Crip
Unapologetic and jaded
Shunned by abled news
Shaped by privileged views
Who he's supposed to be
Where she's supposed to be
What they're supposed to be
A drain on society
A grain of silent compliancy
The irony!
Loud and rebellious
Proud and overzealous
Expectations of us wilt like soggy lettuce
Did you forget us?
Stigmatized
Infantilized
Menace to abled society
Surprised?
Pounding this chest,
King Kong
Flexing his best,
Crip Kong
Chained to stereotypes,
we carry that cross
Elegantly
Flamboyantly
Our culture is boss
Advocating,
celebrating,
graduating,
legislating
Aggravating the status quo.
Educating
We reap what you sow.
Motivating
We rise above the low.
Our imagination,
wild
Our ingenuity,
in style
Venomous
Ravenous
Sensuous
A subtle guile
Look what you've done
Behold!
Your invention
Disabled and proud
Ableism's creation

Healed

The preacher man,
The preacher can
make you walk
with his oil-bathed hand.
They told me that a mustard seed
would make me whole and heal me.
Healing me,
surrounding me,
placing hands
all over me.
Wooden pews
Stained-glass views
Tongues professing,
genuine are few.
Judge my mother, you.
Praise my father, you.
Pity my sister, you.
Unearthed my heathen, you.
Heal me? You can't.
Despite your biblical rant.
Amidst your syllabic chant.
You claim my faith is scant.
I try.
I try harder.

I plea to my master.
I beg and I barter.
Give me legs and I'll run through those pews.
Professing my faith,
spreading the good news.
I'll travel the earth,
nation to nation.
A celebration of my transformation.
Realization.
I open my eyes.
Gone is the preacher and his oil-bathed lies.
Silent are the tongues and their garbled guise.
Hollow are the pews,
stained-glass goodbyes.
Goodbyes to the eyes
that view me as broken.
No longer the leper.
No longer the token.
Imperfectly whole I rule from this chair.
Crippled perfection,
an answered prayer.
Irreverent in spirit, rebellious and unkneeled.
A sinner's reflection of one who is healed.

Dark Side

I like it when the eyes look at me through the lens of pity.
Feel sorry for what they see.
An image that tugs on sympathy.
Unaware of the raw and gritty that occupies the depths of this soul.
They truly don't know.
They don't understand.
That hidden by this chair is the dark side of a man.
With fire that burns.
Vile that churns.
An appetite for vengeance.
Their image I spurn.

I like it when the eyes look at me through the lens of frigidity.
Feel sorry for what she sees.
An image that tugs indifferently.
Unaware of the raw and gritty that waits in the depths of this soul.
She truly doesn't know.
She doesn't understand.
That hidden by this chair is the dark side of a man.
With lust that devours.
Carnality that showers.
An appetite for passion.
Her indifference I scour.

I like it when the eyes look at me through the lens of judgment.
Feel sorry for what he sees.
An image that tugs religiously.
Unaware of the raw and gritty that stirs in the depths of this soul.
He truly doesn't know.
He doesn't understand.
That hidden by this chair is the dark side of a man.
With sacrilege that spears.
Skepticism that smears.
An appetite for unveiling
His judgment disappears.

I like it when the eyes look at me through the lens of uncertainty.
Feel sorry for what you see.
An image that tugs avoidantly.
Unaware of the raw and gritty that screams in the depths of this soul.
You truly don't know.
You don't understand.
That hidden by this chair is the dark side of a man.
With scars that pain.
Journeys that stain.
An appetite for belonging.
Your avoidance I disdain.

Part Three

Dreams, Death, and Visceral Verses

Crip Paradise

I dreamt a dream
of things unseen
Utopia discovered,
a Crip's wild scene
From the corners all four,
en masse they arrived
Queer Crips,
Black Crips,
Brown Crips,
an unapologetic beehive
Signing,
Rolling,
White cane strolling
Breaking out of institutions,
no more controlling
Our minds and bodies rejected by ableds
A new world order,
We turn the tables!
Crip life of oppression
now an old fable
Crip life is in session,
gone are the labels
Crip life is freshened,
ableist stench locked in stables
Music engulfs from Short-e's turntables.
A festive vibe,
colors come alive
Pizarro at his canvas,
creating for the tribe
A cultural revolution
that won't be denied
Mercado, the model
Moore, the poetic scribe
Activists, artists.
Faces, places
A vision so surreal,
words fail to describe.
I dreamt a dream
of things unseen
Utopia discovered,
a Crip's wild scene.

Walls

Hard to love,
I am
Complicated
Isolated
I am
When the dagger strikes
I replicate it
I can.

No mistaking
The silence is aching
It does
The foundation of you, me, is undertaken
by my self-preservation

After all, past sins flood my thoughts
They do
Past hurts, souls were bought
They were
Yesterday's words, a boomerang caught
Fraught
is this heart that plays the part
For authenticity can only replicate tragedy's plot

The invalidness was too much
It is
The brokenness is a crutch
It was
The openness is such,
walls become breath
Filling my lungs with solitude's touch
Guarding my tongue from scars that judge
Keeping me
away from reflection's smudge
They will

You, not me

You.
You saw me.
You saw me sitting.
You saw me sitting in my wheelchair.
You smiled politely.
You smiled politely and walked away.
You walked away to play with your friends.
You walked away to sit with your friends.
You walked away to eat with your friends.

You walked away.

You.
You said hello.
You said hello to me.
You said hello to me daily.
You were interested.
You were interested in me.
You were interested in me and my Cripness.
You felt sorry for me and my "challenges."
You felt sorry for me and my "situation."
You felt sorry for me and my "imperfections."

You felt sorry.

You.
You loved me.
You loved me deeply.
You loved me deeply, unconditionally.
You said yes.
You said yes to life.
You said yes to life together.
You loathed our life together.
You loathed your unconditional love.
You loathed my burden-laced existence.

You loathed me.

You.
You lacked.
You lacked substance.
You lacked substance and courage.
You were afraid.
You were afraid of experiencing.
You were afraid of experiencing Crip's affection.
You existed for you.
You existed for you, your urges.
You existed for you, your urges, your hollowness.

You, not me.

Dear Young Me

Dear young me,

This is future you,
older you.
A wiser you,
black and blue.
Battered and bruised from life's abuse.
The scars will blend with your golden hue.

Let's chat about tomorrow.
Your future, my past. Life's journey for you, constructed to last.
Much longer than you think.
For me,
a flash,
a snapshot,
a transient blink.

Love, lust, intimate affection.
I know you long for that special connection.
A desert of loneliness lined with emptiness.
Empty sex.
Hopefulness.
Forces so strong.
A disastrous mess.
The One will come and bring you joy.
Love.
Memories.
Three images of you fill your legacy.
Journeys, worries, time scurries.
Flurries melt on passion's doom.
Leaving puddles where love once bloomed.
Drowning memories of two.
Killing memories of five.
Stay alive!
Embrace the pain.
Endure the rain.
Resiliency will be born out of heartbreak's remains.
The One will come… again.
Passion, love, blooms… again.

Memories... again.
Puddles... again.

Success is hidden and you're so driven.
Searching for your niche with narrow vision.
No one will steer you.
No one will guide.
No one will see that vision inside.
Burning deep within you.
Yearnings leap within you.
Learning creeps within you.
Earnings steep within you.
Opportunities missed.
Failures kissed.
You'll rise repeatedly.
You'll raise your fist.
Leader, they'll call you.
Vocal, they'll hear you.
Writer, they'll know you.
Activist, outlier.
Injustice will fuel your fire.
Read these words, lyrically penned.
Poetic verses.
From you they stem.

You will sail seas.
Travel foreign lands.
Roam streets with unfamiliar faces.
Sunsets on the sand.

You will be oppressed.
Views of ableist walls.
Roam streets with unfamiliar faces.
Dimly lit halls.

At some point, your body will leave you.
At some point, your father will leave you.
At some point, your sister will leave you.
At some point, life will deceive you.
Believe in you.
The good in you.
The smart in you.

The God in you.
Times that start anew.

How does it end?
Death's door.
A darkness you will see.
Your last breath will be but a pause.
Your reminder of life's fragility.

Lastly, importantly.
Love yourself,
unconditionally.
Forgive yourself,
repeatedly.
Be true to yourself,
infinitely.

Love hard in that chair!
Stand tall in that chair!
Live fierce in that chair!

Love and Peace,

Older you.

Last Breath

Gasp…
deep breath
Lights go dimmer
Grasp, past strength
Thoughts, faux glimmer

Fight, I don't
Let the escape free me
Fight, I won't
Let the dark's tranquility
carry this
shell
far from the pains
of ableism's hell
Far from the stigmas
you've tried to sell
Far from the pandering
and tokenism's bell
Can't you tell?
Exhaustion's veil I wear so well
Discrimination's scar,
my show and tell

Gasp…
fast breath
Eyes get thinner

Grasp…
past depth
Memories, no longer shimmer

Voice,
I can't
Let silence fill the air
Choice,
I rant alone, from my soul's chair
Against the injustice to come,
the oppression that numbs,
the ingestion of pity's hand-fed crumbs
I scream,
I pound
rhythmically on equity's drums
Hoping this beat is played by one
I succumb
The moments, unapologetic
The verses,
poetic
The journey,
prophetic
It is done!

Gasp...
last breath.

Unburied

Bury me not,
at that final hour.
When resistance sleeps,
when I rest in power.
Bury me not,
after the remembrance and goodbyes.
When this body lies still,
when tears flow from eyes.

Bury me not,
for I am not of here.
I am not of there.
This body belongs
to the journeys of this chair.
Scatter the dust,
this art of imperfection.
Scatter, you must,
in every direction.

Allow me to flutter near childhood's call.
Lakeside,
Northside,
The ivy-covered wall.
Plant me on the dirt
where he who named me lays.
On the grounds of academia
where intellect raised.
At the doors of paradise
where the Pacific meets sun's rays.
On Square's lawn
where voices of justice are heard and praised.

Bury me not,
where my heartbeats end.
Permit me to relive,
to fulfill what is penned.

Acknowledgments

I have to start by thanking my favorite person, my love, Michelle. From reading first drafts to providing quiet time and space, she is the beat to the lyrics in this book. Thank you babe!

To the team at POOR Press: thank you so much for believing in me and fostering my work. Lisa "Tiny" Garcia, you are a nugget of knowledge and encouragement whom I'll forever appreciate. Also, much appreciation to my Copy Editor Megan Skelly. Thank you for being my second pair of eyes.

Crip Lyrics would not be the art piece that it is without my talented illustrator, Melissa Marie Eckardt. Thank you so much for sharing your time and beautiful artistry.

Thank you, the reader, for your support. By purchasing my book, you are amplifying the work of disabled artists. Whether this is your first book written by a disabled author or an addition to your Crip library, I am honored that you chose my work.

Finally, to my community, the wonderful Crips/Disabled folks/People with Disabilities, I celebrate the artistry, activism, and passion that embody our beautiful souls! The kinship I have with many of you is deeply treasured. Thank you for encouraging me to share my lived experiences and perspectives through these pages.

www.ingramcontent.com/pod-product-compliance
Lightning Source LLC
Chambersburg PA
CBHW042014150426
43196CB00002B/39